Under the Skin
Badger Plays Book 1

CH00781506

Night Caller
and other plays

Louise Loxton

Contents:

Under the Skin - *The Plays:*

Badger Publishing Limited 15 Wedgwood Gate, Pin Green Industrial Estate,
Stevenage, Hertfordshire SG1 4SU
Telephone: 01438 356907.　　Fax: 01438 747015.
www.badger-publishing.co.uk　　enquiries@badger-publishing.co.uk

Under the Skin - Book 1　　ISBN 1 84424 428 8

Text © Louise Loxton 2005
Series editing © Mike Gould 2005
Complete work © Badger Publishing Limited 2005

All rights reserved. No part of this publication may be reproduced, stored in any
form or by any means mechanical, electronic, recording or otherwise without the
prior permission of the publisher.

The right of Louise Loxton to be identified as author of this Work has been
asserted by her in accordance with the Copyright, Designs and Patents Act 1988.

Series Editor: Mike Gould　　Publisher: David Jamieson
Editor: Paul Martin　　Cover design: Adam Wilmott
Cover illustration: Roger Wade-Walker (Beehive Illustration)

Introduction

Welcome to Badger's *Under the Skin* Book 1!

This collection of five stimulating and challenging plays is designed for enjoyment, but also to help students develop speaking and listening, drama and theatre skills. The series title also gives a clue to the focus for these plays. They may cover a range of ideas, issues, stories and situations, but each is intended to uncover how and why individuals act in the way they do. Thus, these are plays designed with the stage and acting in mind, though they can be equally enjoyed as group readers.

The plays themselves offer a mix of humour and emotion, joy and sadness, triumph and despair, and also cover a wide range of forms and styles. On the one hand, there is *The Gift*, which deals with a family tragedy and how three friends work through difficult feelings. On the other, there is *Night Caller*, which takes a typical situation - the salesman at the front door, and gives it a dramatic and touching twist.

The plays are designed, for the most part, for small groups, ranging from three to five characters, and stage directions are generally kept to a minimum, but are given as a prompt for those who wish to put these on for performance.

All the plays in the series are written by people who are involved, or have been involved, in practical drama work with young people aged 11-16. For this reason, it is hoped that teachers and students will find them compelling and rewarding.

NIGHT CALLER

Characters:

DAVID	aged 13
EDGAR	aged 15
JENNIE	David's sister, aged 12
MUM	

Scene 1   The sitting room

Night. A sitting room in DAVID and JENNIE's home. They are both watching a DVD. There is a coffee table with a phone on it.

DAVID: It's just as good after watching it ten times.

JENNIE: Yeah, I'm so pleased we've got it on DVD.

DAVID: And Mum'll be pleased we're not fighting!

JENNIE: We're not that bad.

DAVID: What d'ya mean? Last week you tried to stab me with that letter opener!

JENNIE: That was just me doing my Gladiator routine - My name is Maximus Jennie-us...

DAVID: Yeah - Russell Crowe's got a lot to answer for. Anyway, hope you're not thinking of modelling yourself on him! (*gestures at screen*)

JENNIE: I dunno - quite fancy myself as a female Terminator.

The doorbell rings.

DAVID: You answer it Jen, it's your turn.

JENNIE: OK, pause the DVD.

Scene 2   The hallway

Lights up on side of stage. JENNIE looks through the 'peephole' before opening the door, but leaves it on the chain. A grimy young man steps into the light, but is obviously 'outside'.

JENNIE: Yeah?

EDGAR: Good evening, miss. My name's Edgar and I have some interesting artefacts for you to peruse...

JENNIE: Eh?

EDGAR: I have a case full of interesting goods, which you may like to look at.

JENNIE: Sorry. Not interested. Goodbye.

She closes the door. The figure stands for a moment at the side of the stage and looks toward the centre. Lights up on the sitting room and as they do, fade lights on the man outside...

DAVID: Who was it?

JENNIE: Oh some grubby looking bloke trying to sell something.

DAVID: What?

JENNIE: Looked like junk to me. Funny name and strange way of speaking too.

DAVID: Good, you got rid of him then. Back to the film.

He flicks the 'pause' button and they resume their viewing.

Scene 3   The sitting room

Later the same evening. The living room.

DAVID: (*standing up and putting the DVD back into its case*) Still a great film. Don't care what people say.

Doorbell is heard ringing.

JENNIE: Your turn this time.

DAVID walks to the same side of the stage as before and goes through the same routine, except that on this occasion he doesn't use the door chain.

DAVID: Yeah?

The same grimy character is on the doorstep as before.

EDGAR: Good evening, sir. My name is Edgar and I have some artefacts which you may like to peruse.

DAVID: You're that same bloke who came earlier, aren't you?

EDGAR: Would sir be interested?

DAVID: Look, give us a break mate...

He moves to close the door but EDGAR steps forward, half into the house.

JENNIE comes out of the living room to see who it is.

JENNIE: You're the same guy!

EDGAR: Indeed, miss. I believe I have some things of interest which I think you will like...

DAVID: Well that's for us to know and you NOT to find out. Get lost.

JENNIE: Wait a moment, David. The guy's clearly desperate.

You got a card or anything? You know. I.D.

EDGAR: I am afraid you have me at a disadvantage.

JENNIE: Never mind. David - let him in.

DAVID: What? Mum'll go mad.

JENNIE: He's harmless. And there's two of us.

DAVID: He won't have anything we want.

EDGAR: How can sir know unless he has a look?

DAVID: Alright. You can come in. ONE minute, and you must promise to stop talking weird.

He opens the door and EDGAR enters.

DAVID: Make this quick.

JENNIE: Yeah, we've got homework to do, and... actually, take your time...

EDGAR: Well, miss, I have some interesting items for you. Let me display them for your consideration.

He sets out a range of unusual items on the hall carpet.

DAVID: (to *JENNIE*) He doesn't change his patter, does he?

JENNIE: (*to DAVID*) And, don't like to say this, but he... well, smells funny. Kind of... like a chimney. Ashes, you know.

DAVID: Huh?

JENNIE: Oh, I don't know! Come on, this has gone on long enough. Get rid of him before Mum comes back.

DAVID: OK. He is kind of... weird.

EDGAR: (*stands up*) Now before you I have a range of Victorian memorabilia which may be of interest to you, ranging from sixpence to half a crown in value.

JENNIE: (*to DAVID*) What's he on about?

DAVID: (*to JENNIE*) Old fashioned money I think. (*to EDGAR*) Now look here mate. We are NOT interested in all this junk.

EDGAR looks disappointed.

EDGAR: But surely sir would be interested in...

DAVID: ...you leaving? Yeah, that's right. Now - hop it.

EDGAR: May I ask one favour?

DAVID: Go on.

EDGAR: Would you be good enough to let me partake of a glass of water. I have travelled far, and...

JENNY: I'll get you one.

She disappears off stage, the other side.
The phone rings in the background.

DAVID: Soon as you've had that drink...

EDGAR: Of course, sir.

DAVID turns round to answer it, back towards the middle of the stage...

EDGAR quietly picks his bag up and steps back into the darkness, vanishing.

At the same time, JENNY reappears with the glass, DAVID re-enters and MUM comes through the open door.

She is surprised to see the front door open with DAVID and JENNIE in the hallway.

MUM: Hi guys. Sorry I'm so late. What's going on here then?

Scene 4   The sitting room

The sitting room. MUM has made a cup of tea and is trying to get some answers from DAVID and JENNIE.

DAVID: So, you didn't see some grubby bloke with a bag?

MUM: No - I didn't! I parked the car and...

JENNIE: You must have. It was the only way out!

MUM: I'm still not happy about you letting some stranger in.

DAVID: He was dead persuasive.

MUM: I bet.

JENNIE: Yeah, but not threatening. Kind of quaint. Like an old man, but young.

MUM: You haven't been drinking that bottle of sherry I got for your gran have you?

DAVID: No! He was there. As plain as the nose on my face.

MUM sighs.

MUM: I knew it was a mistake leaving you on your own with a dodgy film. I should have asked Maggie to look in...

JENNIE: We're sorry, Mum. It won't happen again.

MUM: I'm not even sure it did in the first place. You're not winding me up are you, because I've had a long day and...

DAVID: No!

MUM: Well. It's over now. What about the dishwasher? Did you unload it?

JENNIE and DAVID leap up.

JENNIE: Gotta go. Homework.

She leaves.

MUM: David?

DAVID: Stacks. Piles of it.

He leaves too.

Scene 5   The hallway

The next morning. MUM putting her coat on.

MUM: Come on you guys. You'll be late for school.

JENNIE: (*off-stage*) Nearly there, Mum.

DAVID: (*off-stage*) Coming.

They both enter.

JENNIE: David - do you see what I see?

DAVID moves towards the hall stand.

DAVID: What on earth...?

JENNIE: What do you think it is?

They peer at a strange-looking kitchen utensil which is on the hall stand.

MUM: (*enters*) Oh, you found it. Thanks darling. Thought I'd lost it. Maybe the cleaning lady left it out there by mistake. Put it in the cutlery drawer will you.

                Get your skates on, you'll be late.

JENNIE: Mum, what is it? We've never seen anything like it before.

DAVID: (*gives her a look*) Yes, we have.

MUM: I haven't got time now. Come on, out the door.

She motions for them to move.

DAVID stands still.

DAVID: Just tell us, Mum.

MUM: You must have seen it before. It's always in that odds and ends drawer in the kitchen.

JENNIE: What is it?

MUM: It's a Victorian grapefruit cutter that once belonged to your great-grandmother years ago.

DAVID: What?

MUM: I remember my mother telling me. And her mother told her. It's been passed down the family.

JENNIE: What? The cutter?

MUM: Yes - and the story. You see, this young grubby-looking salesman came to this very door almost one hundred years ago and tried to sell your great-grandmother some kitchen utensils.

JENNIE: Did he smell? Of chimneys?

MUM: Probably. Who knows? But he was certainly not very well turned out.

DAVID: Weird. But why's the story been passed down? Not exactly exciting is it? Grubby bloke sells young lady grapefruit cutter.

MUM: Because that young man turned out to be my grandfather, your great-grandfather!

DAVID and JENNIE look at each with disbelief.

DAVID: Was his name... Edgar?

MUM pauses.

MUM: No - I don't think so. Edward, I think. Anyway, he fell in love at first sight and kept coming back until great-grandma bought something! He was most persistent!

She looks at the cutter and then tosses it to JENNIE.

Put it back in the drawer, love. Don't want to lose it. I'll get the car out.

She leaves.

JENNIE: (*to DAVID*) Do you believe in ghosts?

DAVID: I didn't. But now…

JENNIE: Did it definitely happen?

DAVID: I think so. I mean, yes. But let's just say what we do know.

JENNIE: What's that?

DAVID: We had a night-caller. And we turned him out.

JENNIE: No we didn't. I got him a glass of water. You went to answer the phone. By the way, who was it?

DAVID: Cold call, I think. Line went dead when I picked it up.

JENNIE: Thing is, he - Edgar - chose to leave. So maybe he'll come back.

There's a beep of the car horn.

DAVID: Back to reality. Come on.

They leave.

THE GIFT

Characters: three friends

AMY	aged 13
KATE	aged 14
PAM	aged 14

The stage is set with two basic scenes. On one side the café; on the other a clothes shop. As the action switches between one and the other, the lights fade up and down.

Scene 1   Café

In town on a Saturday afternoon, the three girls are shopping. The scene opens outside 'Café Cadbury'.

KATE: Shall we go for a drink? I'm nearly shopped out.

PAM: No, let's have another 20 minutes in 'New Look' and then call it a day, OK?

AMY: Fine by me.

PAM: Anyway, we've still got to get a pressie for your birthday next week, Amy. Nearly as old as Kate and me now!

AMY: Don't worry - I'm not fussed about pressies.

KATE: Oh come on, Amy. We want to buy you something.

AMY: OK - I'll meet you back here when you're done. I'll grab a hot chocolate or something.

PAM: Fine. See ya.

KATE: See ya in a mo.

Scene 2   New Look

KATE and PAM are in 'New Look'.

PAM: I've actually not got much dosh left. Have you, Kate?

KATE: (*empties her purse - coins rattle out*) Three pounds, and forty... oooh, wait a minute! (*she shakes her purse - a single coin falls out*) Three pounds forty-five, actually...

PAM: Well I've got a fiver. Shall we put our money together and buy Amy something jointly?

KATE: Good thinking.

PAM: I'll check that 'Sale' box - bound to be something in there.

KATE: I'll check the sale rail.

PAM: OK. Meet you at the checkout in ten.

Scene 3   Café

*Lights up on AMY, who is sitting in 'Café Cadbury' at a
table by herself. She has a large cup of hot chocolate by
her side and there's a chocolate biscuit on a plate. She is
writing in a diary, but she speaks the following lines.
Any other characters in the café should remain seated as
she speaks to the audience.*

AMY: (*writing*) Dear Diary,

I wish I'd had the guts to tell Pam and Kate
the truth about my birthday. It's not that I
don't want to celebrate it, and I know that
Dad is organising something special
secretly, but it just won't be the same.

This will be the first celebration - the first
family do - since the funeral, and all I want
to do is curl and up and hide away.

And now I'm sitting here pretending to be
as cool as I can. Let's hope Pam and Kate
don't cotton on to how I'm feeling.

She closes the book.

Scene 4   New Look

Back in 'New Look', at the checkout. KATE and PAM compare their bargains.

KATE: Hey, what you got Pam?

PAM: (*holds item up*) What d'you think? It's black, it's see-through and it's well cool. Guess how much? £2.99! Think she'll like it?

KATE: Like it? Is the Pope Catholic? Is Justin Timberlake a hunk? Is my dad old? Is...?

PAM: OK, I get the idea.

KATE: I'm gonna get one too.

PAM: Bad luck. I got the last one. What did you get?

KATE: I found these. (*she holds up a pair of black cropped jeans*) They were more expensive. £4.99!

PAM: Amazing - we've got her a new outfit for under £8! Trini and Susannah - eat your heart out! Think we should give it her early?

KATE: Cool. She'll be so chuffed. Plus she seems kind of... I don't know...

PAM: Quiet?

KATE: Yeah. I dunno. Something.

PAM: This'll cheer her up, then, won't it?

Scene 5   Café

PAM and KATE sitting with AMY in 'Café Cadbury'.
They're sipping hot chocolates.

PAM: You not having another, Amy?

AMY: I've had three! Twenty minutes, you said.

KATE: Pam needed a wee.

AMY: Must have been a big one.

PAM: How was I to know the toilets were the other side of town?

AMY: So, how did you get on?

PAM: They were surprisingly clean.

AMY: Not the toilets!

KATE: Oh, the shops were OK. Pass me that cake, Pam.

PAM: These are really yummy, aren't they?

AMY: Yeah, it's the marshmallows on top I like.

PAM: Anyway, apart from the toilets, we had great success in 'New Look'.

AMY: Oh.

PAM: Don't get too excited, Amy.

AMY: Sorry...

KATE: (*excited*) Yeah, we've got you a joint pressie. We'd like to give it to you now, if that's OK?

AMY: Honestly, you guys, it's very nice of you but...

PAM: Don't be so nice. You should say: where's my present? I demand my present!

AMY: Sorry.

PAM: And stop saying 'sorry'. Or 'but'! When you see it, you'll *love* it.

KATE: She might not. She might have bad taste. You never know.

PAM: Take no notice, Amy - you'll adore it...

They pass her the bag.

KATE: Here you are, Amy, from Pam and me for your fourteenth birthday.

They start singing 'Happy Birthday to you...'

AMY opens her present and bursts into tears.

PAM and KATE stop singing.

PAM: OK. We admit it. They were in the sale. They were cheap. We're cheap!

AMY: It's not that. It's... they're... lovely...

KATE: You OK?

PAM: Tell us what's wrong.

KATE: C'mon Amy. We're your mates.

PAM puts her arm around her shoulders. KATE pulls her own chair closer.

What's the matter, you poor ol' thing?

PAM: In your own time, Amy...

AMY: (*sobbing*) I'm sorry... didn't mean it...

KATE: Of course you didn't...

AMY: (*still sobbing*) The presents are great...

PAM: Yeah, you'll look fab in them.

AMY: (*still tearful*) It's just that when I opened the bag, all I saw was 'black'...

KATE: A great colour on you...

AMY: I know it's stupid. But it reminded me of Mum's funeral... (*AMY bursts into tears again*) I can't seem to get the pictures out of my head.

KATE and PAM look at each other in shock.

KATE: The last thing we wanted to do was upset you.

PAM: Shall we take them back?

KATE: We could try to get another colour.

AMY: No thanks, honest. Changing the clothes won't change me.

27

PAM: You need another hot chocolate. I'll get you one.

KATE: (*hisses*) We haven't got any money!

PAM: I'll tell the manager it's an emergency. I can be very persuasive.

She gets up and goes.

AMY hands her diary to KATE while PAM orders the drinks.

KATE: What's this?

AMY: I can't... I mean sometimes it's easier to write than speak...

KATE: Can I read it?

AMY: Yes. It might make sense of my tears.

KATE reads the diary entry and PAM returns to the table with the drink.

PAM: Here you are.

AMY: Thanks.

PAM: What are you reading, Kate?

AMY: Let Pam read it too.

KATE hands the diary to PAM.

KATE: I didn't realise.

PAM reads the diary entry, then closes it and puts it down on the table.

PAM: Amy, you poor ol' thing...

AMY: (*trying to smile*) Not till next Thursday.

KATE: See? That's better already. You made a joke.

PAM: Why didn't you tell us you were still so upset about your mum?

AMY: It's not the sort of thing people want to hear about. Besides I've talked and talked about it with Dad, with my relations, with... well everyone. It doesn't do any good. It doesn't go away.

KATE: But we're your friends, Amy. It's different with us.

PAM: Maybe Amy's right.

KATE: Huh? I'm looking for some support here!

PAM: Well it is difficult to talk about death. Or rather to talk to the right people.

KATE: Hello? What can be more right than friends and family?

PAM: I mean someone... I dunno. Uninvolved. Like the school nurse.

AMY: I've tried that. No good at all.

PAM: Well maybe she could suggest a counsellor.

AMY: That's for psychos. I'm not mad.

KATE: (*interrupting*) Hang on a minute, Amy, that's not fair.

PAM: Kate saw the school counsellor when her dad left her mum, didn't you?

KATE: Yeah. I know it wasn't death. Nothing like that. But if felt kinda similar.

AMY: I'm sorry, Kate. I didn't mean it...

KATE: No worries. I know you didn't. So, what d'you think?

AMY: The black jeans and top? Yeah. They're cool.

KATE: No - Pam's idea.

AMY: I'll give it a try.

She gets up.

KATE: Where you going? I thought things were...

AMY: Toilet. Four hot chocolates are more than anyone can take. Pam, you want to come and check them out? You're the expert!

KATE: Don't be too long. That manager bloke keeps on giving me filthy looks.

PAM: I'm not surprised. I told him you were paying.

Lights down.

BOYS BEHAVING BADLY

Characters:

PHIL	13
SPENCER	14
MATT	14
MIKE	14
MR CRAWLEY	A school teacher on duty

Scene 1   The school playground

Tuesday. The school playground. PHIL, SPENCER and MATT are having a cigarette behind the bike sheds. Enter MIKE.

MIKE: So, this is where you girlies are hiding. I had my fag walking over here. Easy as pie. Just hide it in your hands.

Anyway, what are you lot doing at the weekend?

MATT: I'm off to see my auntie who's down from Scotland.

SPENCER: I'm supposed to be working at the veggie shop.

PHIL: (*to Mike*) Why? What are you thinking of?

MIKE: My mum's away this weekend. Thought I'd get you guys round for a few cans and the footie Saturday night. Then whatever we wanna do afterwards.

PHIL: I'm not getting in any nicked cars.

MIKE: Calm down, Phyllis. All I'm talking about is a few friendly drinks, a few fags and a bit of footie. What d'ya think?

MATT: Dunno 'bout me mate. Auntie Annie's expected Saturday.

MIKE: Auntie Annie? You're the Auntie Annie! You can get out of work early, Spence, can't you?

SPENCER: Not too sure, I'll see what I can do.

PHIL: Will you tell your mum that we're sleeping over?

MIKE: (*fixes him with cold look*) What d'ya think I am, stupid?

PHIL: I just thought... I mean my parents would like to know if my mates were coming over.

MIKE: I'm sure they would, Mr Goody Two Shoes! So, I can count you out then?

PHIL: I didn't say that... it's just...

MIKE: Are you up for it or not?

PHIL: Yeah. Definitely maybe. I mean, I am. Up for it, that is.

The bell goes for afternoon lessons.

MIKE: Well you two other girlies let me know, alright. I'll get us in some bevvies, OK? Lights out! Creepy Crawley's heading this way...

Scene 2   Bus stop

Friday morning. MATT and SPENCER are waiting for the school bus.

SPENCER: So, you going to Mike's tomorrow then?

MATT: No can do. Me mum's organised a family do for me auntie and that's that!

SPENCER: Me neither. I've been grounded.

MATT: Why's that?

SPENCER: 'Coz of my report last week. Usual stuff, blah, blah, poor homework, not enough care, blah blah too much time working in the shop...

MATT: Yeah, I've heard that tune before. Mine wasn't that good either.

SPENCER: Dad said if I wanna work, no more nights out.

Bus approaches.

MATT: Hey, let's push in and get this one, I can
see Mike coming. I don't wanna talk to him.

Scene 3   School playground

*Friday breaktime. School playground. PHIL, MATT and
SPENCER are chatting.*

PHIL: Looks like tomorrow night's off for you guys
then?

SPENCER: Yeah, Mike's not gonna like it.

MATT: Nothing I can do, I'm afraid.

SPENCER: Maybe I could sneak out. The boss is hardly
ever there.

PHIL: You reckon?

SPENCER: Why not? The rules are there to be broken.

PHIL: What about your earnings - thought you
were skint?

SPENCER: Look, what's your problem? That's my
business!

PHIL: Hey Spence, don't have a go at me, I'm just thinking of your bank balance!

SPENCER: Yeah, sorry mate - I'd just love a night out, that's all. Just not sure I wanna spend it with Mike the Nutter.

MATT: Me too - but no way can I get out of this one.

PHIL: Well, what about we put our heads together and present Mike with an alternative? Cos he's not gonna like it if we're not there. You know how he gets.

MATT: Such as? A night with Auntie Annie at my place?!

I can just see it. Oh, Mike, would you mind passing me the mayonnaise? Oh and can you put on 'Songs of Praise' for me...?

PHIL: That's Sunday night.

MATT: Whatever. You get my point.

PHIL: Yeah. Guess so. What do you suggest?

SPENCER: Yeah... let's think.

Scene 4   School gates

End of school, Friday. PHIL, SPENCER and MATT are at the school gates.

PHIL: Here he comes.

MIKE ambles along carrying a heavy bag - he's obviously stocked up for the match.

MIKE: Right there. So, you all made arrangements, right? Cos you've been avoiding me all day, you lot. I'll see you at seven tomorrow, OK?

MATT: No can do mate. Sorry. (*he shuffles his feet and looks at the ground*)

MIKE: You serious, you wimp?

MATT: Sorry Mike. It's...

MIKE: You'll be the sorry one, I've just spent a fortune on our entertainment.

He moves towards MATT to punch him. PHIL intervenes and MIKE drops his bag. The cans spill out on the floor, some burst open.

Look what you've done. Hurry and pick 'em up before Creepy Crawley see us. I'll be dead if he sees. I'm on my last warning...

MATT bends down to pick up the cans.

SPENCER: Don't Matt.

MATT stops.

> (*to MIKE*) You sort it out. You're the one who picked on Matt.

MIKE: (*in disbelief*) What did you say?

SPENCER: All I said was...

MIKE: You trying to pick a fight? (*he moves towards SPENCER in a threatening way*)

PHIL: Oi! You lot - Crawley's on his way...

Scene 5　　　School gates

CRAWLEY: Well, well. If it isn't the three musketeers and their leader. What's going on here, then?

PHIL, SPENCER and MATT look sheepish and stare at the floor.

> (*turning to MIKE*) I presume these cans are yours? And where, may I ask, did you get them?

MIKE: They're ours. Not mine.

CRAWLEY: Is that right? Well?

The others remain silent.

> Doesn't look like your sidekicks are going to back you up.

MIKE: Lads. Say something.

CRAWLEY: I think you've got a lot of explaining to do to the Head, young man. Pick them up and follow me.

MIKE picks up the cans and stuffs them into his rucksack, scowling at the other three.

> And cut the glaring look. Your bullying is well-known.

CRAWLEY marches MIKE off in the direction of the Head's office.

MATT: I didn't mean to let you down, Spence.

SPENCER: You didn't. I've never stood up to him before. Don't know what came over me. I'm an idiot. He'll kill me.

PHIL: No, he won't. Besides, he's alright really.

MATT: No, he's not. He's a headcase.

SPENCER: Mike got what he deserved, Phil.

              We should celebrate. After all, it's the end
              of the week. And we can deal with Mike on
              Monday.

MATT: How we gonna deal with him?

SPENCER: No idea. Take each game as it comes.

PHIL: What?

SPENCER: You know - it's what football managers say.
              Don't look ahead.

MATT: Suits me. So, how we gonna celebrate
              getting him off our backs for a few days.

SPENCER: Well. I know this off-licence that'll serve
              us...

SLEEPING EASY

Characters:

JAMIE	16
GARY	15, his friend
LIAM	23, a Big Issue seller
STUART	22, his friend, also a Big Issue seller
SERGEANT BLAKE	40, a local policeman/woman

Scene 1   A hill above town

Evening. GARY and JAMIE gaze down.

JAMIE: Just look at all that grot hanging in the air. Why did they build a road here?

GARY: Well, no road, no tourists, J.

JAMIE: I just hate the fact that we breathe in so much of it.

GARY: You'd like to live out of town then?

JAMIE: Dunno... People in the country always seem so much more... well... caring, to me.

GARY: Have you forgotten about last Christmas?

JAMIE: Last Christmas?

Dim lights.

Scene 2   Under the bridge

The scene changes to reveal a bridge by a canal. LIAM and STUART placing their sleeping bags on the ground.

LIAM: What a lousy day! I mean, sleeping rough just before Christmas!

STUART: It's not as though we're tramps, is it? I mean, we are trying to get our act together.

LIAM: People don't understand what selling 'The Big Issue' is all about.

STUART: The kids are the worst. Don't schools teach them anything?

LIAM: Yeah, mate. Abuse. A few coins and we'd have been OK. It's freezing!

They settle down on the ground.

STUART: How much did you make?

LIAM: Not enough. It's never enough.

STUART: Night mate. Sweet dreams.

LIAM: Dreams? More like nightmares.

Lights fade slowly.

Scene 3   Under the bridge

Later the same night. Lights up on LIAM and STUART sleeping.

Enter JAMIE and GARY. They have clearly been drinking.

JAMIE: 'Ere mate, watch out! (*JAMIE grabs GARY as he trips over LIAM and nearly falls into the canal!*) Fancy a swim, do you?

GARY: Cheers pal. Don't fancy paddling in the pond tonight!

JAMIE: Just think. All our exams over.

GARY: Till the next ones.

JAMIE: What d'you have to say that for? I'm celebrating!

He swigs from a can and chucks it into the canal. As he does so, he stumbles once again over the two sleepers on the ground.

                Hey, are these a couple of 'grungies'?

LIAM: Oi you! Leave it out. What do you think you're playing at?

He leaps to his feet and JAMIE staggers backwards.
STUART wakes up and GARY lurches backwards.
General confusion. Eventually, all four face each other.

STUART: (*angry*) What's going on?

JAMIE: (*nervously*) Sorry... we didn't see you lying there.

STUART: Right. We're flippin' invisible.

LIAM: You should watch where you're going. Leave us in peace. Not much to ask for after the day we've had.

JAMIE: Who are you? Why are you here anyway?

STUART: It's simple. We didn't have enough money.

GARY: What d'you mean?

STUART: Look, we haven't got time for a maths lesson, mate.

JAMIE: Your parents chuck you out?

LIAM: Just get lost and leave us alone.

JAMIE: Fair enough. Come on Gaz...

GARY: Hang on. I've seen you in town.

STUART: You're a genius.

GARY: You're 'Big Issue' sellers. I remember an assembly we had at school, don't you J?

JAMIE: Yeah, something about them trying to get back on the straight and narrow...

GARY: And trying to get a place to live...

LIAM: (*shouting*) YEAH, BY BEING LEFT ALONE!

GARY: You sell the magazine to raise money, or something...

STUART: You've got it! We are not the 'grungies' you thought we were. Now why don't you get back to your cosy homes?

GARY: Sorry mate, I didn't mean to insult you. Here.

He pulls a scrunched up note from his jacket.

It's only a fiver. S'all I got left.

JAMIE: Wait. I've got a bit too.

He empties his pockets. Coins tumble to the ground. He gathers them up. The two boys hold out their offerings.

STUART: What d'you reckon, Liam?

LIAM: Might get us into somewhere for the night.

STUART: Not sure I want charity from these losers.

LIAM: Losers? What does that make us?

They look at the outstretched hands. For a moment the stage is still and we can see the two pairs facing each other.

The lights fade.

Scene 4   Under the bridge

Later. The same place on the banks of the canal. Suddenly a bright torch is shone on the group.

BLAKE: What's this then? A nice little party or what?

STUART: We're just on our way to the night shelter

BLAKE: Thinking of walking?

LIAM: No - my Ferrari's just round the corner.

BLAKE: Shelter'll be shut by the time you arrive.

STUART: How about a lift then?

BLAKE: Why not? It's not a night for a cat to be out in.

STUART: Thanks Sergeant.

LIAM: I'm bloody freezing!

BLAKE: (*to JAMIE and GARY, both swaying slightly*) Who are you two? You been drinking? You look under age.

STUART: No - that's us. Had a bottle of scotch to warm us up. Punter gave it us.

BLAKE: (*suspicious*) You sure? Who are they then?

LIAM: They're...

STUART: ...mates.

BLAKE: Do they speak?

GARY: Yes officer. Sorry officer. We'll be off now.

JAMIE: What? I was just...

GARY: (*urgently*) Come on!

They leave.

BLAKE: You sure they were mates?

LIAM: Yeah.

BLAKE: If you say so.

He gestures at the sleeping bags.

Right lads. Better get your stuff. The car's round the corner.

STUART: You got a CD player?

BLAKE: Yeah. May not be a Ferrari, but the sound system's top of the range! Let's be off.

Scene 5   A hill above town

As Scene 1. Summer.

GARY: Remember? We got those two blokes a bed for the night. We're no angels, but just cos we live down there doesn't make us different. We shouldn't beat ourselves up over it.

JAMIE: Yeah, I guess.

GARY: I think we're lucky.

JAMIE: Lucky? You seen the pile of homework I've got?

GARY: You know what I mean. I mean, that could have been us.

JAMIE: Us?

GARY: Those two blokes.

JAMIE: That'll never be us.

GARY: That's why we're lucky.

He starts to leave.

Come on, I'll buy you a coke. And a copy of the 'Big Issue'.

JAMIE: Where from?

GARY: There's a guy in town, stands by the bank. I talk to him now and again.

JAMIE: What's his name?

GARY: You'll know him. He's a mate.

They exit. Lights down.

BATH TIME

Characters:

LOUISE   15

ALISTAIR   17, her boyfriend

ROMAN SOLDIER

Scene 1   Central Bath

The scene should suggest the outside of the Roman Baths. Late at night. LOUISE and ALISTAIR enter.

LOUISE: I wonder what it's like in there at night?

ALISTAIR: Bet it's as boring as it is in the day time.

LOUISE: Huh?

ALISTAIR: You know, history. Dull stuff that used to happen. Only plus point is no tourists!

LOUISE: I like looking at ruins.

ALISTAIR: Didn't know you'd met my dad.

LOUISE: Don't be so stupid! Anyway, bet it's dead spooky.

ALISTAIR: Old bricks and smelly water. It's not exactly the Blair Witch Project, is it?

He stops.

Anyway, where has this sudden interest come from?

LOUISE: Ever since I did a project on the Romans in Year 7 actually. I've always found them interesting.

ALISTAIR: Bored me stiff. And now I'm annoyed too.

LOUISE: How come?

ALISTAIR: All the money the council are spending on the Spa project. Waste of time and energy.

LOUISE: Yeah. Guess you're right. These projects take forever.

ALISTAIR: And I don't want to visit them when they do open.

LOUISE: You know something?

ALISTAIR: What?

LOUISE: You are ignorant.

ALISTAIR: What's that mean?

LOUISE: Proves my point. (*suddenly, she grabs him by the arm*)

ALISTAIR: Oh, I see - trying to be all nice now, are you?

LOUISE: No! Look. (*she points off stage*)

ALISTAIR: I can't see anything.

LOUISE: There's a light. In the Baths. Do you think anyone's in there?

ALISTAIR: Workmen probably.

LOUISE: What? 11pm on a Sunday?

ALISTAIR: A workman whose watch is broken?

LOUISE: No - something's up.

ALISTAIR: Yes - I'm cold, it's late, and...

He starts to move off.

LOUISE: Wait! I can see someone moving around. Can you hear that? A strange noise, like metal rattling?

ALISTAIR: Blimey, what an imagination!

LOUISE: (*suddenly*) I'm gonna climb over the wall.

ALISTAIR: What? Are you mad?

LOUISE: It's dead easy. I'll have a quick glance. If there's anything dodgy I'll call the police on my mobile.

ALISTAIR: Why wait? Phone now.

LOUISE: They won't come. Not cos some light is on.

ALISTAIR: What about that rattling sound?

LOUISE: They'll think I'm nuts.

ALISTAIR: You are nuts. Come on, you're not going in there.

He starts to leave, then turns. LOUISE has gone.

ALISTAIR: Louise?

He looks around the stage.

I don't believe it!

He exits in the same direction.

Scene 2   Inside the Baths

Lights up. Inside the Roman Baths. A pale light. Enter ALISTAIR and LOUISE.

ALISTAIR: Great idea, Lou. Well done.

He stops.

ALISTAIR: I'm staying here.

LOUISE: Don't be such a baby - follow me.

ALISTAIR: Only if you hold my hand.

LOUISE: I don't need to hold your hand.

ALISTAIR: It's not you I'm worried about.

LOUISE: Oh I see. Is this the same guy who said it was just a few bricks and smelly water?

She looks at him.

You OK?

ALISTAIR: Yeah, just a bit spooked I suppose.

LOUISE: (*trying to lighten the mood*) Bet you didn't think we'd be in here at midnight when you asked me to go see a film, did you?

ALISTAIR: (*shivers*) What do you think? Come on, let's go. There's nothing here.

LOUISE: Listen! Can't you hear that sound? It's coming from over there...

LOUISE moves to one side of the stage. ALISTAIR follows. They both walk into the wall and half-tumble over each other.

ALISTAIR: Ow! That hurt. Remind me again - why are we doing this?

LOUISE: Ssshhh! It's that noise. Stand still.

They both listen. A faint, dragging metallic sound can be heard.

ALISTAIR: That's it. Lou, I've had enough. Come on, we're outta here.

LOUISE: No way! I'm finding out what's going on. I'll go through the door into the next chamber.

ALISTAIR: You can't go on your own.

LOUISE: Look if anyone comes, you can watch out.

ALISTAIR: Not sure we should split up. In horror films when they do that, it usually means... (*he mimes cutting his own throat*)

LOUISE: Thanks, Ali. That's made me feel better.

ALISTAIR: Exactly. Stay here.

LOUISE: No - I've got to do this. Don't ask me why. You wait here and I'll be back in no time.

ALISTAIR: (*sighing*) OK.

Scene 3   Inside the Baths

A new chamber. Same dim light as before. There is the huge steaming Great Roman Bath. There is no sound except the lapping of the water against the edge of the pool. LOUISE moves around the Bath, taking care not to slip.

LOUISE: There's nothing in here at all…

ALISTAIR: (*from offstage, in a loud whisper*)
Louise, you OK? What's going on in there?

LOUISE: (*whispering*) It's alright. There's nothing here.

Suddenly an enormous figure comes from behind LOUISE and grabs her. She gasps and struggles. ALISTAIR calls out.

ALISTAIR: (*still offstage but nearer*) Louise, what is it? I'm coming through.

He races onto the stage.

LOUISE is struggling with a dark figure.

ALISTAIR: Oi, you brute! Leave her alone!

He searches around the floor, sees a loose brick and picks it up.

LOUISE: Don't throw that. You'll hit me!

She continues to struggle. ALISTAIR drops the brick. He comes to her aid, but the figure throws them both off, casting them onto the floor. Then it seems to slide into the Great Bath, disappearing into the water.

LOUISE clutches ALISTAIR.

LOUISE: How stupid of me. Who was that?

ALISTAIR: Let's not wait to find out. It certainly wasn't any late night workman.

LOUISE: Come on.

They exit.

Scene 4   Library

The next day. The local library. LOUISE sitting at a table with a large book. Enter ALISTAIR.

ALISTAIR: You OK? Still look a bit pale to me.

LOUISE: I'm alright. What about you?

ALISTAIR: Oh, couldn't sleep, had nightmares when I could and woke up in a cold sweat - otherwise fine.

LOUISE: We could've been in big trouble last night.

ALISTAIR: We were in big trouble, or didn't you
                notice?

LOUISE: No - I mean with the police. Imagine trying
                to explain to a copper about that strange
                figure.

ALISTAIR: They'd've thought we'd been drinking!

He sits down.

                You found anything yet?

LOUISE: Yeah. The librarian was dead helpful. Guess
                what I found out?

ALISTAIR: The librarian is really Kylie Minogue in
                disguise?

LOUISE: Be serious.

ALISTAIR: I dunno. How am I supposed to guess?

LOUISE: Alright, I'll tell you.

She jabs a finger at the book in front of her.

ALISTAIR: I can't read that. It's Latin.

LOUISE: Neither can I. But the librarian can and she said it's about some soldier called Caius Caligula who came to Bath.

ALISTAIR: Yawn. Sounds like school to me.

LOUISE: I haven't finished. Point is, he'd just finished a battle and he came back to Bath to get his wife, but she'd vanished.

ALISTAIR: So?

LOUISE: Come on. Even you can see the connection. He looked everywhere, but she couldn't be found.

ALISTAIR: (*slowly understanding*) It was him! The ghost was Caius looking for his wife!

LOUISE: Spot on. Apparently, the ghost is pretty well-known for roaming the Baths at night.

ALISTAIR: They should have a sign up, warning people.

LOUISE: Beware the ghost? He doesn't exist but he might attack you?

ALISTAIR: Something like that. Anyway, seemed pretty real to me.

LOUISE: Me too.

ALISTAIR: Spooksville!

LOUISE: Thank goodness we got out OK.

ALISTAIR: No more bright ideas in the dark!

He shuts the book and stands up.

LOUISE: Too right. And no more Romans, Latins or Italians for me.

ALISTAIR: Come on, let's go for a cappuccino.

They start walking.

LOUISE: Did you say 'cappuccino'?

ALISTAIR: Yeah, why?

LOUISE: Just there's a great coffee-bar near the Baths. Does a wicked cappuccino...

ALISTAIR looks at her.

OK. It was just an idea...

They leave. They walk out of the library towards a local café. Lights dim.